TROMSØ TRAVEL GUIDE 2025

Experience Norway's Unforgettable Arctic Journey.

DARRELL KENNEDY

© 2025 by Darrell Kennedy. All rights reserved.

No part of this book may be reproduced, distributed, or transmitted in any form or by any means, including photocopying, recording, or other electronic or mechanical methods, without the prior written permission of the author, except in the case of brief quotations embodied in critical reviews and certain other non-commercial uses permitted by copyright law.

This book is a work of non-fiction. The author has made every effort to ensure the accuracy and completeness of the information contained herein. However, the author assumes no responsibility for errors, omissions, or damages resulting from the use of the information. The author is not liable for any loss or injury caused by the use of this book. The views and opinions expressed in this book are those of the author and do not necessarily reflect the official policy or position of any organization or entity.

TABLE OF CONTENTS.

CHAPTER 1: INTRODUCTION 6
- Welcome to Tromsø 9
- Why Visit Tromsø? 10
- Overview of Tromsø 12

CHAPTER 2: PLANNING YOUR TRIP 14
- Best Time to Visit 14
- Events and Festivals 19
- Travel Tips and Essentials 20
- Entry Requirements and Visas 21

CHAPTER 3: GETTING THERE 25
- Air Travel to Tromsø 25
- Alternative Travel Options 29
- Transportation from the Airport ... 34

CHAPTER 4: WHERE TO STAY 39
- Budget Accommodations 39
- Budget-Friendly Hotels 44
- Mid-Range Hotels 46
- Luxury Lodgings 53
- Unique Experiences 56

CHAPTER 5: THINGS TO DO 57

Northern Lights Viewing 57

Outdoor Activities 61

Cultural Experiences 72

Day Trips and Excursions 79

CHAPTER 6: LOCAL DINING 81

Top Restaurants 81

Local Cuisine 87

CHAPTER 7: PRACTICAL TIPS 91

What to Pack 91

Weather and Safety 92

Local Transportation 94

Useful Phrases in Norwegian 100

CHAPTER 9: BONUS 103

Map Guides 103

One week Itinerary 112

CONCLUSION 114

Scan To Discover More Captivating Travel Guides for Your Next Journey.

CHAPTER 1: INTRODUCTION

The Arctic wind whipped through my hair as I stood on the deck of the Hurtigruten, the midnight sun painting the sky in hues of gold and pink. Mountains rose like jagged teeth from the icy waters, their peaks dusted with snow even in July.

This was Tromsø – a city at the edge of the world, where the Northern Lights dance across the winter sky and the sun refuses to set in summer.

I first arrived in Tromsø with a backpack and a thirst for adventure. I spent weeks exploring its charming streets, hiking its rugged trails, and marveling at the natural wonders that surrounded me.

I kayaked through serene fjords, stood in awe beneath the Arctic Cathedral, and sipped strong coffee in cozy cafes while snow fell softly outside.

I chased the elusive Aurora Borealis, my breath catching in my throat as the sky erupted in a symphony of green and purple.

Tromsø captivated me with its raw beauty, its vibrant culture, and the warmth of its people. It's a place where you can feel truly alive, where the boundaries between civilization and wilderness blur, and where adventure awaits around every corner.

This guide is an invitation to discover Tromsø for yourself. Whether you're seeking the thrill of dog sledding through snowy landscapes, the serenity of a Northern Lights cruise, or the simple pleasure of exploring a city steeped in history and charm, Tromsø has something to offer everyone.

Within these pages, you'll find everything you need to plan your own unforgettable journey to this Arctic paradise. From practical tips on getting there and finding the perfect accommodation to insider recommendations on the best places to eat, drink, and explore, I'll be your guide to unlocking the magic of Tromsø.

Get ready to embark on an adventure that will stay with you long after you've left this captivating city at the edge of the world.

Welcome to Tromsø

Imagine a city bathed in the ethereal glow of the Aurora Borealis, where snow-dusted mountains meet the icy expanse of the Arctic Sea. This is Tromsø, a vibrant metropolis nestled 350 kilometers north of the Arctic Circle, a place where modern life harmonizes with the raw beauty of the Arctic wilderness.

Known as the "Gateway to the Arctic," Tromsø is a city of contrasts. Here, cutting-edge architecture stands alongside historic wooden houses, and a thriving cultural scene pulsates beneath the mesmerizing dance of the Northern Lights.

This unique blend of urban energy and natural splendor makes Tromsø a truly captivating destination.

Tromsø's history is deeply intertwined with the Arctic. Vikings first settled here over a thousand years ago, laying the foundation for a city that would become a vital hub for explorers, fishermen, and traders. Today, Tromsø remains a key center for Arctic research and a gateway for expeditions to the polar regions.

But Tromsø is more than just a base for adventure. It's a city with a soul, where you can wander through charming streets lined with colorful houses, discover fascinating museums that tell tales of polar exploration and Sami culture, and savor the flavors of the Arctic in world-class restaurants.

Why Visit Tromsø?

Tromsø offers a unique blend of experiences that you won't find anywhere else:

- Witness the magic of the Northern Lights: Tromsø is renowned as one of the best places in the world to witness the Aurora Borealis. From September to April, the night sky often comes alive with a breathtaking display of dancing lights, a spectacle that will leave you in awe.
- Immerse yourself in Arctic landscapes: Surrounded by majestic fjords, snow-capped mountains, and pristine islands, Tromsø is a paradise for nature lovers. Explore dramatic landscapes, hike scenic trails, or embark on a boat trip to discover hidden coves and encounter Arctic wildlife.
- Embrace the spirit of adventure: Whether you're seeking adrenaline-pumping activities or tranquil moments in nature, Tromsø has something for everyone. Go dog

sledding through snowy forests, kayak in the fjords under the midnight sun, or try your hand at ice fishing.
- Delve into Sami culture: Learn about the indigenous Sami people, their rich traditions, and their deep connection to the land. Visit a Sami village, experience reindeer sledding, and discover their unique artistry and craftsmanship.
- Indulge in Arctic flavors: Tromsø's culinary scene is a delightful fusion of traditional and modern. Savor fresh seafood caught in the icy waters, sample reindeer dishes, and enjoy locally sourced ingredients in innovative restaurants.
- Experience the warmth of Arctic hospitality: The people of Tromsø are known for their friendly and welcoming nature. You'll find a relaxed atmosphere and a genuine sense of community, making your visit even more enjoyable.

Overview of Tromsø

Tromsø is situated on Tromsøya island, connected to the mainland by the iconic Tromsø Bridge, a graceful arch that has become a symbol of the city.

The city center, with its colorful wooden houses and bustling pedestrian streets, is compact and easily explored on foot.

Key districts and landmarks:

- Tromsø City Center: The heart of Tromsø, this area is home to historic buildings, shops, restaurants, and cultural attractions. Don't miss the Tromsø Cathedral, the oldest Protestant church in Northern Norway.

- The Harbor: A bustling hub of activity, the harbor is where you'll find ferries, fishing boats, and tour operators. It's also a great place to enjoy waterfront views and fresh seafood.
- Prestvannet: This picturesque lake, located just south of the city center, is a popular spot for recreation and Northern Lights viewing.
- Tromsdalen: Across the Tromsø Bridge lies Tromsdalen, home to the striking Arctic Cathedral, a modern architectural masterpiece with a distinctive triangular shape.
- Telegrafbukta: This popular beach area offers stunning views of the mountains and is a great place to relax, swim (in the summer!), or enjoy a picnic.

CHAPTER 2: PLANNING YOUR TRIP

Best Time to Visit

Tromsø, bathed in the ethereal glow of the Aurora Borealis or the Midnight Sun, offers a unique experience no matter when you choose to visit.

However, each season paints a different picture of this Arctic city, with its own set of advantages and drawbacks.

Winter (November – March): Embrace the Arctic Magic

As the polar night descends and the sun dips below the horizon, Tromsø transforms into a winter wonderland. This is the time to witness the mesmerizing dance of the Northern Lights, a spectacle that will leave you breathless.

Pros:

- Northern Lights: Peak viewing season for the Aurora Borealis, with dark, clear skies offering optimal conditions.
- Winter Activities: Embrace the Arctic spirit with thrilling experiences like dog sledding, snowmobiling, skiing, and snowshoeing.
- Festive Atmosphere: Enjoy the cozy ambiance of Christmas markets, festive decorations, and the warmth of local cafes.

Cons:

- Limited Daylight: Experience the polar night, with only a few hours of twilight each day. This can limit outdoor activities and sightseeing.
- Cold Temperatures: Be prepared for freezing temperatures and pack accordingly with warm layers, waterproof outerwear, and sturdy footwear.
- Peak Season: Winter is a popular time to visit, so expect higher prices for flights and accommodation. Book well in advance.

Spring (April – May): Awakening of the Arctic

Spring brings a sense of renewal to Tromsø, as the sun climbs higher in the sky and the days grow longer. The landscape begins to thaw, revealing a tapestry of vibrant colors.

Pros:

- Increasing Daylight: Enjoy longer days with more sunlight, allowing for extended outdoor adventures.
- Milder Temperatures: Experience more comfortable temperatures, making it pleasant for hiking and exploring.
- Shoulder Season: Benefit from fewer crowds and potentially lower prices compared to peak season.

Cons:

- Unpredictable Weather: Spring can bring a mix of sunshine, rain, and even snow. Be prepared for variable conditions.
- Limited Accessibility: Some attractions and activities may still be closed or have limited operating hours.

- Mud Season: Melting snow can create muddy conditions on trails and roads, so be prepared for some mess.

Summer (June – August): Land of the Midnight Sun

Tromsø basks in the glow of the Midnight Sun, a surreal phenomenon where the sun never sets. Experience endless days filled with outdoor adventures and a vibrant atmosphere.

Pros:

- Midnight Sun: Witness the magical phenomenon of the sun staying above the horizon 24 hours a day.
- Long Days: Maximize your time with extended daylight hours, perfect for hiking, kayaking, and exploring.
- Festivals and Events: Enjoy a lively atmosphere with various cultural events, music festivals, and outdoor activities.

Cons:

- Peak Season: Summer is the busiest time to visit Tromsø, so expect higher prices and larger crowds.
- No Northern Lights: The Midnight Sun makes it impossible to see the Aurora Borealis during this time.
- Limited Availability: Accommodation and tours can book up quickly, so plan and reserve well in advance.

Autumn (September – October): Autumnal Hues and Auroral Displays

Autumn casts a spellbinding charm over Tromsø, as the landscape transforms into a canvas of fiery reds, oranges, and yellows. The nights grow longer, offering another chance to witness the Northern Lights.

Pros:

- Fall Foliage: Admire the breathtaking beauty of autumn colors painting the mountains and valleys.
- Northern Lights: Enjoy another opportunity to see the Aurora Borealis with the return of darker nights.
- Fewer Crowds: Experience a more tranquil atmosphere with fewer tourists compared to peak season.

Cons:

- Unpredictable Weather: Autumn can bring rain, wind, and the first snowfall. Be prepared for changing conditions.
- Shorter Days: Daylight hours decrease as winter approaches, limiting outdoor activities.
- Limited Accessibility: Some attractions and tours may start to reduce their operating hours or close for the season.

Events and Festivals

Tromsø's calendar is filled with vibrant festivals and events throughout the year, offering a glimpse into the city's rich culture and traditions. Here are a few highlights:

- Tromsø International Film Festival (January): A renowned film festival showcasing a diverse range of international and Arctic cinema.
- Sami Week (February): Celebrate the indigenous Sami culture with traditional music, food, and events.
- Nordlysfestivalen (Northern Lights Festival) (January/February): A music festival featuring classical, jazz, and contemporary performances inspired by the Aurora Borealis.

- Midnight Sun Marathon (June): A unique marathon experience running under the Midnight Sun.
- Bukta Open Air Festival (July): A popular music festival featuring rock, pop, and indie artists.
- Tromsø Arctic Pride (October): A celebration of LGBTQ+ rights and culture.

By considering the distinct characteristics of each season and the timing of special events, you can plan a Tromsø adventure that perfectly aligns with your interests and desires.

Travel Tips and Essentials

A trip to Tromsø requires a bit more preparation than your average getaway. Here's a breakdown of essential information to ensure a smooth and enjoyable experience in the Arctic:

Money Matters

- Currency: Norway's currency is the Norwegian Krone (NOK). While credit cards are widely accepted, it's always a good idea to have some local currency on hand, especially for smaller shops, markets, and transportation.
- ATMs: ATMs are readily available throughout Tromsø. Look for ATMs marked with the "BankAxept" logo for the widest network.
- Credit Cards: Major credit cards like Visa and Mastercard are widely accepted. However, American Express and Diners Club may have limited acceptance.
- Currency Exchange: Currency exchange services can be found at the airport, banks, and some hotels. However, ATMs generally offer better exchange rates.
- Tipping: Tipping is not expected in Norway, as service charges are usually included in the bill. However, rounding up the bill or leaving a small tip for exceptional service is appreciated.

Entry Requirements and Visas

- Passport: Ensure your passport is valid for at least six months beyond your intended stay in Norway.
- Schengen Visa: Norway is part of the Schengen Area. If you are a citizen of a country that requires a visa to enter the Schengen Area, you will need to obtain a Schengen visa

before your trip. Check the Norwegian Directorate of Immigration website for the most up-to-date visa requirements and application procedures.

- Visa-Free Travel: Citizens of many countries can enter Norway for tourism or business purposes for up to 90 days without a visa. However, it's crucial to confirm your specific visa requirements based on your nationality.

Travel Insurance: Don't Leave Home Without It

Comprehensive travel insurance is essential for any trip, especially to a destination like Tromsø where weather conditions can be unpredictable and activities can involve some risk.

- Coverage: Ensure your policy covers medical expenses, trip cancellation or interruption, baggage loss or delay, and personal liability.
- Activities: If you plan on participating in adventure activities like skiing, dog sledding, or snowmobiling, make sure your insurance covers these activities specifically.
- Emergency Contact: Keep your insurance policy information readily accessible and inform a family member or friend of your policy details.

Packing Essentials: Be Prepared for Arctic Conditions

Packing for Tromsø requires careful consideration of the season and your planned activities. Here's a general packing list:

Warm Clothing:

- Base Layers: Thermal underwear, long-sleeved shirts, and leggings.
- Mid-Layers: Fleece jackets, wool sweaters, and down vests.
- Outer Layers: Waterproof and windproof jacket and pants.
- Accessories: Warm hat, gloves, scarf, and thick socks.

Footwear:

- Waterproof Boots: Sturdy, insulated, and waterproof boots with good grip are essential for winter conditions.
- Comfortable Shoes: Pack comfortable walking shoes or hiking boots for exploring the city and surrounding areas.

Other Essentials:

- Waterproof Gear: Pack a waterproof backpack or dry bag to protect your belongings from rain or snow.
- Sunglasses: Even in winter, the sun can be strong, especially when reflecting off the snow.
- Sunscreen: Protect your skin from the sun's rays, even on cloudy days.
- Swimsuit: If you plan on visiting a sauna or thermal baths.
- Daypack: A smaller backpack for day trips and excursions.

Electronics and Other Necessities

- Adapters: Norway uses European-style plugs (Type F). Bring a travel adapter if your devices use a different plug type.
- Phone Charger: Don't forget your phone charger and any necessary cables.
- Medications: Pack any prescription medications you need, along with a copy of your prescription.
- First-Aid Kit: A basic first-aid kit with essentials like bandages, pain relievers, and antiseptic wipes.
- Headlamp or Flashlight: Useful for navigating dark winter days or evenings.

CHAPTER 3: GETTING THERE

Air Travel to Tromsø

For most travelers, the journey to Tromsø begins at Tromsø Airport (TOS), a modern and efficient gateway to the Arctic. Located on the island of Tromsøya, just a short distance from the city center, the airport offers a seamless arrival experience and convenient connections to destinations across Norway and beyond.

Tromsø Airport (TOS): Your Arctic Gateway

Location: Tromsø Airport is situated at Langnes, on the western part of Tromsøya island, approximately 5 kilometers (3 miles) from the city center.

Terminals: The airport has two main terminals:

- Terminal A: The newer and larger terminal, handling most scheduled flights and international arrivals. It features

modern facilities, including check-in desks, baggage claims areas, shops, restaurants, and a duty-free store.
- Terminal B: The older terminal, primarily used for regional flights operated by Widerøe. It offers basic amenities such as check-in counters and waiting areas.

Airlines Served: Tromsø Airport is well-connected to major cities in Norway and several international destinations. Major airlines operating at the airport include:

- SAS (Scandinavian Airlines): Offers frequent flights to Oslo and other Norwegian cities, as well as international destinations like Copenhagen and Stockholm.
- Norwegian Air Shuttle: Operates domestic flights within Norway and select international routes, including London-Gatwick.
- Widerøe: Connects Tromsø to various regional airports in northern Norway, providing access to smaller towns and communities.
- Other Airlines: Several other airlines offer seasonal or charter flights to Tromsø, including Lufthansa, KLM, Finnair, and easyJet.

Navigating the Airport

- Arrival: Upon arrival, follow the signs for baggage claim and customs. If you have nothing to declare, proceed through the green channel.

- Customs and Immigration: Non-EU/EEA citizens may need to present a valid passport and visa (if required). Be prepared to answer questions about the purpose and duration of your visit.
- Departure: Check in for your flight at the designated counters in Terminal A or B. Allow ample time for security checks and boarding procedures.

- Facilities: Tromsø Airport offers a range of amenities for travelers, including:
- Shops and Duty-Free: Browse a selection of souvenirs, gifts, and travel essentials.
- Restaurants and Cafes: Enjoy a meal or a quick snack before your flight.
- Currency Exchange: Exchange currency at the airport if needed.
- Tourist Information: Obtain maps, brochures, and helpful information from the tourist information desk.
- Wi-Fi: Free Wi-Fi is available throughout the airport.

Domestic and International Flight Connections

Domestic Flights: Tromsø Airport serves as a major hub for domestic travel within Norway. Frequent flights connect Tromsø to cities like Oslo, Bergen, Trondheim, Bodø, and other destinations in northern Norway.

International Flights: Tromsø offers direct flights to several international destinations, including:

- London-Gatwick (LGW): Operated by Norwegian Air Shuttle.
- Other European Cities: Seasonal flights may be available to other European cities, such as Berlin, Gdansk, and Kraków.

Connecting Flights: For destinations not served by direct flights, Tromsø Airport offers convenient connections through Oslo Airport (OSL), which serves as a major international hub.

Alternative Travel Options

While flying is the most common way to reach Tromsø, adventurous souls and those seeking a more scenic journey have other compelling options to consider.

Hurtigruten Coastal Ferry: A Voyage Through Majestic Landscapes

For a truly unforgettable experience, consider embarking on a Hurtigruten coastal ferry journey. Often referred to as "the most beautiful voyage in the world," Hurtigruten offers a unique way to travel along the Norwegian coast, with Tromsø as one of its key ports of call.

- The Route: Hurtigruten operates daily sailings along the Norwegian coast, connecting 34 ports from Bergen in the south to Kirkenes in the north (and vice versa). The journey to Tromsø offers breathtaking scenery, including dramatic fjords, towering mountains, charming coastal towns, and possibly even glimpses of wildlife like whales and sea eagles.

Why Choose Hurtigruten?

- Scenic Beauty: Immerse yourself in the stunning landscapes of Norway's coastline.
- Unique Experience: Combine transportation with a cruise-like experience, enjoying onboard amenities and excursions.
- Port Exploration: Hop on and off at various ports to explore different towns and cities along the route.
- Variety of Itineraries: Choose from different routes and durations to suit your travel plans.

Things to Consider:

- Travel Time: The journey to Tromsø can take several days, depending on your starting point.
- Cost: Hurtigruten can be more expensive than flying, especially if you opt for a cabin with a view.
- Seasickness: If you're prone to seasickness, be prepared with medication or consider alternative travel options.

Driving: Embark on a Scenic Road Trip

For those who enjoy the freedom and flexibility of the open road, driving to Tromsø can be a rewarding adventure. However, be prepared for long distances, varying road conditions, and potential winter driving challenges.

Driving Routes:

- From Southern Norway: The E6 highway is the main north-south artery, offering stunning views of fjords, mountains, and forests.
- From Finland or Sweden: Cross-border routes are available, but be aware of potential winter road closures.

Road Conditions:

- Summer: Generally good road conditions, but be mindful of narrow roads, tunnels, and occasional road work.

- Winter: Winter driving in Norway can be challenging, with snow, ice, and limited daylight. Winter tires are mandatory, and chains may be required in some areas. Check road conditions before you go and be prepared for potential delays.

Car Rental:

- Several car rental companies operate in Tromsø and other major cities. Book in advance, especially during peak season.
- Consider renting a vehicle with four-wheel drive or winter tires for added safety and traction in winter conditions.

Things to Consider:

- Driving Distances: Be prepared for long driving distances, especially if traveling from southern Norway.
- Fuel Costs: Fuel prices in Norway can be high, so factor this into your budget.
- Ferries: Some routes may require ferry crossings, so check schedules and fares in advance.
- Winter Driving: Exercise caution and be prepared for challenging conditions if driving in winter.

Bus and Train: Limited but Scenic Options

While bus and train travel to Tromsø is possible, it's generally less convenient and more time-consuming than flying or driving. However, these options can offer scenic routes and a chance to experience more of Norway's landscape.

Bus:

- Long-distance buses connect Tromsø with other major cities in Norway.
- Check routes, schedules, and fares with companies like NorWay Bussekspress.

Train:

- There is no direct train connection to Tromsø. The closest train station is in Narvik, which is then connected to Tromsø by bus.
- This option is more suitable for travelers who want to combine train travel with other modes of transportation.

Transportation from the Airport

Tromsø Airport (TOS), located on the island of Langnes, is your gateway to this Arctic city. Once you've collected your luggage and cleared customs, several convenient transportation options are available to whisk you away to your Tromsø adventure.

Airport Express Bus: A Swift and Scenic Ride

The Flybussen Airport Express Coach offers a direct and efficient connection between the airport and the city center.

With comfortable seating and ample luggage space, it's a popular choice for travelers seeking a hassle-free journey.

Route: The bus follows a scenic route, passing through residential areas and offering glimpses of the surrounding mountains and fjords. It makes several stops along the way, including major hotels and the city center.

Frequency: Buses depart approximately every 20 minutes, with increased frequency during peak hours and after flight arrivals.

Ticket Prices:

- Adults: NOK 100 (approximately $9.50 USD)
- Children (4-15 years): NOK 50 (approximately $4.75 USD)
- Children under 4: Free

Where to buy tickets:

- Online: Pre-book your tickets on the Flybussen website (www.flybussen.no) for a discounted fare.
- Onboard: Purchase tickets directly from the bus driver (cash or card accepted).
- Ticket Machines: Automated ticket machines are available at the airport and some bus stops.
- Travel Time: The journey to the city center takes approximately 15-20 minutes, depending on traffic.

Taxis: Door-to-Door Convenience

For those seeking a more personalized and direct transfer, taxis are readily available outside the airport terminal.

Availability: Taxis are typically waiting at the designated taxi rank outside the arrivals hall.

Fares: Expect to pay around NOK 200-250 (approximately $19-$24 USD) for a ride to the city center. Fares may be higher during evenings, weekends, and holidays.

Pre-booking Options: If you prefer to have a taxi waiting for you upon arrival, several companies offer pre-booking services:

- Tromsø Taxi: +47 03011
- Din Taxi: +47 02045

Tips:

- It's common to round up the fare to the nearest 10 NOK as a tip.
- If you have a lot of luggage or are traveling in a group, consider booking a larger taxi or minivan in advance.

Car Rentals: Explore at Your Own Pace

Renting a car provides the freedom and flexibility to explore Tromsø and its surroundings at your own pace.

Several car rental companies operate at the airport, offering a variety of vehicles to suit your needs.

Companies:

- Avis
- Budget
- Europcar

- Hertz
- Sixt

Tips:

- Book your rental car in advance, especially during peak season.
- Consider your driving experience in winter conditions if you plan to visit during the snowy months. Winter tires are mandatory.
- Familiarize yourself with Norwegian driving rules and regulations.
- Parking in Tromsø city center can be limited and expensive.

Important Notes

- Luggage: All transportation options mentioned above accommodate luggage.
- Accessibility: The Airport Express bus and taxis are wheelchair accessible. If you require accessible transportation, inform the service provider in advance.
- Travel Time: Travel times can vary depending on traffic and weather conditions.

CHAPTER 4: WHERE TO STAY

Budget Accommodations

Finding comfortable and affordable accommodation is key to enjoying your Arctic adventure without breaking the bank.

Tromsø offers a variety of budget-friendly options, each with its own unique charm and atmosphere.

Hostels

Tromsø Activities Hostel: This hostel is a vibrant hub for social butterflies and adventure seekers. It's known for its friendly atmosphere and organized activities, making it easy to connect with fellow travelers.

Key features:

- Social Vibe: Regular events like pub crawls, movie nights, and Northern Lights chases foster a sense of community.

- Comfortable Common Areas: Relax and socialize in the spacious common room, complete with comfy couches, a TV, and board games.
- Well-Equipped Kitchen: Prepare your own meals in the fully equipped communal kitchen, saving money on dining out.

- Variety of Rooms: Choose from dorms (4-10 beds) or private rooms with shared or ensuite bathrooms.
- Free Wi-Fi: Stay connected with free high-speed Wi-Fi throughout the hostel.
- Central Location: Situated in the heart of Tromsø, within walking distance of major attractions, shops, and restaurants.
- Location: Storgata 107, Tromsø
- Approximate price: Dorms from NOK 300, private rooms from NOK 800.

Enter Backpack Hotel: This modern hostel blends style and affordability, offering a comfortable and social environment for travelers.

Key features:

- Rooftop Terrace: Enjoy panoramic city views from the rooftop terrace, perfect for socializing or soaking up the midnight sun.
- Modern Design: Stylish and contemporary décor creates a welcoming and comfortable atmosphere.
- Game Room: Challenge your fellow travelers to a game of pool, foosball, or board games in the dedicated game room.
- Guest Kitchen: Prepare your meals in the well-equipped guest kitchen, complete with all necessary appliances and utensils.
- Secure Lockers: Keep your valuables safe in individual lockers provided in each dorm room.

- Central Location: Located just steps away from the harbor, offering easy access to ferries, tours, and city attractions.
- Location: Parkgata 4, Tromsø
- Approximate price: Dorms from NOK 350, private rooms from NOK 900.

Guesthouses

AMI Hotel: This family-run guesthouse offers a warm and personalized experience, making you feel right at home.

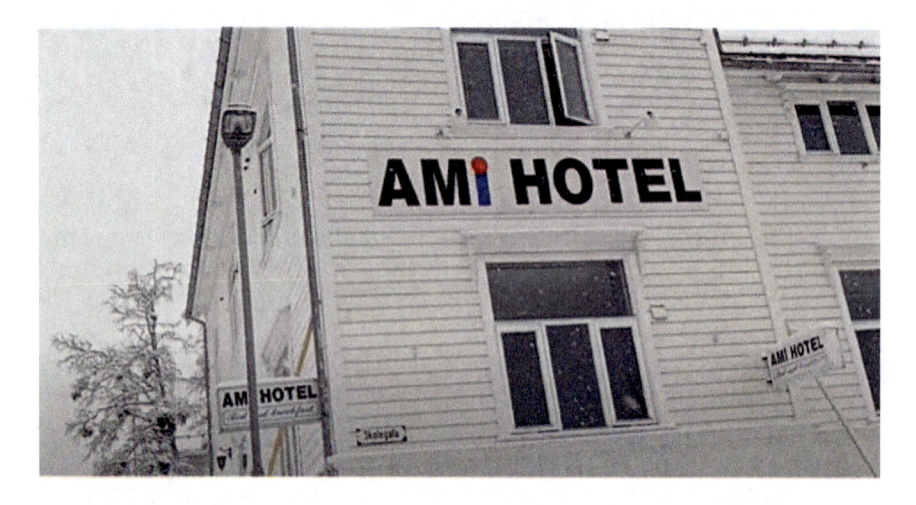

Key features:

- Homely Atmosphere: Experience the genuine hospitality of the friendly owners who go the extra mile to ensure a pleasant stay.
- Comfortable Rooms: Simply furnished but cozy rooms provide a restful retreat after a day of exploring.

- Shared Kitchen: Prepare your own meals and snacks in the shared kitchen, equipped with a fridge, stove, and basic utensils.
- TV Lounge: Relax and unwind in the communal TV lounge, a perfect spot to meet other guests.
- Free Wi-Fi: Stay connected with complimentary Wi-Fi throughout the guesthouse.
- Central Location: Situated in the city center, close to shops, restaurants, and public transportation.
- Location: Skolegata 24, Tromsø
- Approximate price: Single rooms from NOK 600, double rooms from NOK 800.

Boukersen Heim: This charming guesthouse offers a tranquil escape from the city bustle, nestled in a quiet residential area.

Key features:

- Peaceful Setting: Enjoy a relaxing stay in a quiet neighborhood, surrounded by greenery and away from the city noise.
- Spacious Rooms: Comfortable rooms with shared bathroom facilities offer ample space and natural light.
- Communal Kitchen: Prepare your own meals in the fully equipped communal kitchen, fostering a sense of community among guests.

- Beautiful Garden: Relax and unwind in the peaceful garden, a perfect spot to enjoy a cup of coffee or read a book.
- Free Wi-Fi: Stay connected with complimentary Wi-Fi access throughout the guesthouse.
- Residential Location: Located a short bus ride or a pleasant walk from the city center, offering a peaceful retreat.
- Location: Kirkegårdsveien 41, Tromsø
- Approximate price: Single rooms from NOK 550, double rooms from NOK 750.

Budget-Friendly Hotels

Smarthotel Tromsø: This modern hotel offers a stylish and efficient stay without the hefty price tag.

Key features:

- Contemporary Design: Enjoy a modern and stylish environment with a focus on functionality and comfort.

- Compact Rooms: Well-designed rooms maximize space and offer essential amenities for a comfortable stay.
- Free Wi-Fi: Stay connected with complimentary high-speed Wi-Fi throughout the hotel.
- 24-Hour Reception: Benefit from 24-hour reception service for assistance and convenience.
- Breakfast Buffet: Start your day with a delicious breakfast buffet (available for an additional fee).
- Central Location: Located in the heart of Tromsø, within walking distance of major attractions and the harbor.
- Location: Vestregata 6, Tromsø
- Approximate price: Single rooms from NOK 700, double rooms from NOK 900.

Comfort Hotel Xpress Tromsø: This trendy hotel caters to independent travelers who appreciate a minimalist design and self-service options.

Key features:

- Trendy Vibe: Experience a modern and vibrant atmosphere with a focus on self-sufficiency and convenience.
- Comfortable Rooms: Relax in comfortable rooms equipped with essential amenities and modern décor.
- Free Wi-Fi: Stay connected with complimentary Wi-Fi throughout the hotel.

- Vending Machines: Enjoy 24/7 access to snacks and drinks from vending machines located on each floor.
- Breakfast Bags: Grab a convenient breakfast bag to go (available for an additional fee).
- Central Location: Situated in the city center, close to shops, restaurants, and public transportation.
- Location: Grønnegata 35, Tromsø
- Approximate price: Single rooms from NOK 650, double rooms from NOK 850.

Mid-Range Hotels

Scandic Ishavshotel

Steeped in history and overlooking the breathtaking Tromsø harbor, the Scandic Ishavshotel offers a unique blend of old-world charm and modern comforts.

This iconic landmark, established in 1866, has welcomed explorers, adventurers, and travelers for over a century.

Key Features:

Unbeatable Location: Situated directly on the harborfront, the hotel provides stunning views of the waterfront, the Arctic Cathedral, and the surrounding mountains. It's within easy walking distance of the city center, shops, restaurants, and the departure point for many tours and excursions.

Historical Ambiance: Experience a touch of Tromsø's past in this historic building, with its elegant architecture and preserved features. The hotel seamlessly blends its heritage with modern amenities, creating a unique and charming atmosphere.

Variety of Rooms: Choose from a range of comfortable and well-appointed rooms, including standard rooms, superior rooms with harbor views, and spacious family rooms. All rooms feature modern amenities like flat-screen TVs, free Wi-Fi, and comfortable beds.

Culinary Delights: Indulge in delicious meals at the hotel's on-site restaurant, which offers a menu featuring fresh, local ingredients and stunning harbor views. Unwind with a drink at the cozy bar, a perfect spot to socialize or enjoy the ambiance.

Wellness Facilities: Maintain your fitness routine in the well-equipped fitness center, complete with cardio machines and weights. Afterward, relax and rejuvenate in the sauna, offering panoramic views of the city.

Family-Friendly: The hotel caters to families with a dedicated children's play area, spacious family rooms, and babysitting services (upon request).

Approximate price: NOK 1,200 – 2,000 per night.

Clarion Collection Hotel Aurora

The Clarion Collection Hotel Aurora provides a warm and inviting atmosphere in the heart of Tromsø. This stylish hotel focuses on personalized service and creating a cozy home-away-from-home experience for its guests.

Key Features:

Central Convenience: Located in the city center, the hotel offers easy access to shops, restaurants, cultural attractions, and public transportation. Explore Tromsø's vibrant streets and discover hidden gems right at your doorstep.

Complimentary Evening Buffet: Enjoy a delicious and complimentary evening buffet featuring a variety of hot and cold dishes, salads, and desserts. This value-added offering allows you to savor local flavors and socialize with other guests.

Relaxing Lounge Area: Unwind in the comfortable lounge area, complete with a fireplace, comfortable seating, and a selection of books and magazines. It's the perfect spot to relax after a day of exploring or enjoy a quiet evening.

Modern and Comfortable Rooms: The hotel offers a variety of well-appointed rooms with comfortable beds, modern amenities like flat-screen TVs and free Wi-Fi, and stylish décor. Choose from standard rooms, superior rooms, or junior suites for added space and comfort.

Pet-Friendly Policy: Traveling with your furry companion? The Clarion Collection Hotel Aurora welcomes pets, making it an ideal choice for pet owners. (Pet fees may apply, so be sure to inquire when booking.)

Approximate price: NOK 1,100 – 1,800 per night.

Thon Hotel Polar

The Thon Hotel Polar offers a modern and functional stay in a convenient location.

This hotel caters to both leisure and business travelers, providing comfortable accommodations and essential amenities for a pleasant stay.

Key Features:

Fitness Facilities: Maintain your fitness routine while traveling in the hotel's well-equipped fitness room, featuring cardio machines, weights, and other exercise equipment.

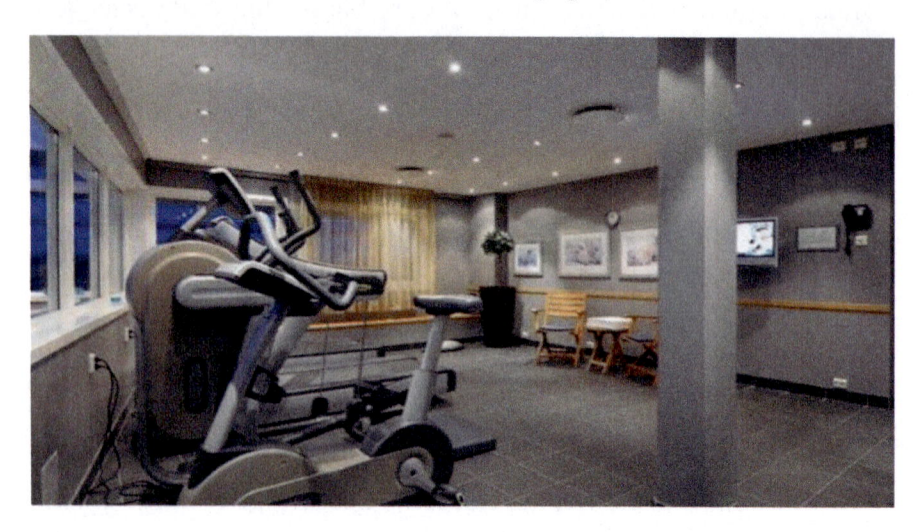

City Center Location: Situated near Storgata, Tromsø's main shopping street, the hotel provides easy access to a variety of shops, restaurants, cafes, and public transportation options. Explore the city's vibrant atmosphere right at your doorstep.

Hearty Breakfast Buffet: Start your day with a delicious and energizing breakfast buffet featuring a wide selection of hot and cold dishes, pastries, fruits, and beverages. It's the perfect way to fuel up for a day of sightseeing or activities.

Business-Friendly: The hotel offers conference facilities and meeting rooms, making it a suitable choice for business travelers. Stay connected with free Wi-Fi and utilize the business center for printing and other services.

Comfortable and Functional Rooms: The hotel offers a range of modern and functional rooms, each equipped with comfortable beds, work desks, flat-screen TVs, and free Wi-Fi. Choose from standard rooms, superior rooms, or family rooms to suit your needs.

Approximate price: NOK 1,000 – 1,600 per night.

Radisson Blu Hotel Tromsø

The Radisson Blu Hotel Tromsø provides a reliable and comfortable stay with a touch of Scandinavian elegance.

This international hotel chain offers a consistent standard of service and amenities, ensuring a pleasant experience for travelers.

Key Features:

Spectacular Waterfront Views: Enjoy breathtaking views of the Tromsø harbor, the surrounding mountains, and the Arctic Cathedral from many of the hotel's rooms and its on-site restaurant. Wake up to stunning scenery and soak in the beauty of the Arctic landscape.

Culinary Experiences: Savor delicious meals at the hotel's restaurant, which features a menu highlighting fresh, local ingredients and Scandinavian flavors. Unwind with a drink at the stylish bar, offering a relaxed atmosphere and panoramic views.

Wellness and Relaxation: Maintain your fitness routine in the well-equipped fitness center, featuring a variety of cardio and strength-training equipment. Afterward, relax and rejuvenate in the sauna, offering a tranquil escape.

Business Amenities: The hotel caters to business travelers with a dedicated business center offering printing, copying, fax services, and meeting rooms. Stay connected with free Wi-Fi throughout the hotel.

Spacious and Well-Appointed Rooms: Enjoy a comfortable stay in spacious and well-appointed rooms, each featuring modern amenities like flat-screen TVs, free Wi-Fi, comfortable beds, and work desks. Choose from standard rooms, superior rooms with harbor views, or suites for added luxury.

Approximate price: NOK 1,300 – 2,200 per night.

Luxury Lodgings

Clarion Hotel the Edge: This contemporary waterfront hotel boasts stunning views of the harbor and mountains. Indulge in their luxurious amenities, including a rooftop terrace with a sauna and hot tub, a gourmet restaurant featuring fresh, local ingredients, and stylish rooms with floor-to-ceiling windows.

- Address: Kaigata 6, 9008 Tromsø

- Website: [https://www.nordicchoicehotels.com/hotels/norway/tromso/clarion-hotel-the-edge/] (https://www.nordicchoicehotels.com/hotels/norway/tromso/clarion-hotel-the-edge/)
- Highlights: Infinity pool, fitness center, on-site bar, meeting facilities.

Enter St. Elisabeth Suites & Spa: Experience true indulgence at this elegant hotel. Enjoy spacious suites with private balconies, a state-of-the-art spa with a range of treatments (massages, facials, aromatherapy), and fine dining options with an emphasis on regional specialties. The hotel's central location provides easy access to Tromsø's attractions.

- Address: Mellomvegen 50, 9007 Tromsø
- Highlights: 24-hour room service, concierge service, library, in-room fireplaces (in some suites).

Scandic Ishavshotel: This iconic hotel, known for its distinctive architecture resembling ice floes, offers panoramic views of the city, harbor, and surrounding mountains.

Relax in their comfortable rooms with modern Scandinavian design, savor delicious meals at their restaurant with a focus on Arctic cuisine, and unwind in the sauna with breathtaking views.

- Address: Fredrik Langes gate 2, 9008 Tromsø
- Website: [https://www.scandichotels.com/hotels/norway/tromso/scandic-ishavshotel] (https://www.scandichotels.com/hotels/norway/tromso/scandic-ishavshotel)
- Highlights: Family-friendly rooms, pet-friendly options, sustainable practices.

Tromsø Ice Domes Hotel: (Seasonal – December to March) For a truly unique experience, spend a night in a luxurious ice dome. These beautifully sculpted accommodations feature intricate ice carvings, cozy reindeer hides, and thermal sleeping bags to keep you warm. Enjoy the ice bar with its ice sculptures and the magical atmosphere.

- Location: Tamokdalen (about 90 minutes from Tromsø city center by car)
- Website: [https://www.tromsoicedomes.com/] (https://www.tromsoicedomes.com/)
- Highlights: Guided tours of the ice domes, dog sledding and snowshoeing excursions, chance to see the Northern Lights.

Unique Experiences

Sami Lavvu Stay: Immerse yourself in the indigenous Sami culture by spending a night in a traditional lavvu (tent). Learn about Sami traditions, enjoy a meal cooked over an open fire (like bidos, a traditional reindeer stew), and perhaps even witness the Northern Lights dancing above you.

- Provider Example: Tromsø Arctic Reindeer Experience
- Address: Reindeer camp located in Tamokdalen valley (approximately a 1-hour drive from Tromsø)
- Website: https://www.tromsoarcticreindeer.com/
- Activities: Lavvu stays, reindeer sledding, lasso throwing, Sami cultural presentations, Northern Lights viewing.

Cabin in the Wilderness: Escape the city and reconnect with nature in a secluded cabin. Enjoy the tranquility of the Arctic wilderness, go hiking or fishing, and savor the peace and quiet.

Many cabins offer amenities like wood-burning stoves, private saunas, and stunning views of the fjords or mountains.

- Booking Platforms: Airbnb, Booking.com (search for "cabins near Tromsø")
- Tip: Look for cabins on Kvaløya Island, Sommarøy Island, or in the Lyngen Alps for scenic locations.

Lighthouse Accommodation: Stay in a historic lighthouse and experience life as a keeper of the coast. Enjoy breathtaking views of the sea, observe marine life, and learn about the fascinating history of these maritime landmarks.

- Provider Example: Sommarøy Arctic Hotel
- Address: Sommarøy, 9110 Hillesøy (on Sommarøy Island, about a 1.5-hour drive from Tromsø)
- Website: [https://www.sommaroy.no/] (https://www.sommaroy.no/)
- Features: Modern rooms in a converted lighthouse, restaurant with sea views, opportunities for kayaking, hiking, and fishing.

CHAPTER 5: THINGS TO DO

Northern Lights Viewing

Tromsø, located within the auroral zone, is renowned as one of the best places in the world to witness the mesmerizing Northern Lights (Aurora Borealis).

This natural phenomenon occurs when charged particles from the sun collide with atoms in the Earth's atmosphere, creating a breathtaking display of dancing lights.

Best Time to See the Northern Lights

The Northern Lights are visible in Tromsø from late August to mid-April, during the dark winter months. The optimal viewing time is between 6:00 PM and 2:00 AM, when the sky is at its darkest.

Factors that Influence Visibility:

- Clear Skies: Cloud cover will obscure the Northern Lights, so check the weather forecast for clear nights.
- Solar Activity: The intensity of the Northern Lights depends on solar activity. You can monitor space weather forecasts for predictions of auroral activity.
- Light Pollution: Get away from city lights for the best viewing experience.

Popular Viewing Spots Around Tromsø

- Prestvannet Lake: This easily accessible lake just outside the city center offers a dark sky and reflections of the Northern Lights on the water.
- Tromsø Ice Domes: (Seasonal) The Ice Domes provide a unique setting for Northern Lights viewing, away from light pollution. They often organize guided tours.
- Fjellheisen Cable Car: Take the cable car up to Storsteinen mountain for panoramic views of the city and the

surrounding area, increasing your chances of seeing the aurora.
- Telegrafbukta Beach: This beach south of Tromsø offers a wide-open sky and less light pollution than the city center.
- Kvaløya Island: This island, accessible by car or bus, offers several spots with minimal light pollution, such as Grøtfjord and Kattfjord.

Northern Lights Tours and Cruises

Several tour operators in Tromsø offer guided Northern Lights experiences:

- Bus Tours: These tours take you to locations outside the city with optimal viewing conditions. They often provide warm clothing, hot drinks, and photography tips.
- Mini-bus Tours: Smaller groups and more personalized experiences.
- Northern Lights Cruises: Enjoy the aurora from the water, away from light pollution, with the added possibility of seeing marine wildlife.
- Dog Sledding or Snowmobiling Tours: Combine Northern Lights viewing with an adventurous activity.

Tips for Photographing the Northern Lights

- Use a Tripod: A stable tripod is essential for capturing sharp images of the aurora.
- Manual Settings: Set your camera to manual mode and experiment with different ISO, aperture, and shutter speed settings. A wide aperture (low f-number) and a high ISO will help capture more light.
- Focus to Infinity: Set your lens to manual focus and focus to infinity.
- Remote Shutter Release or Timer: Use a remote shutter release or the camera's timer to avoid camera shake.
- Extra Batteries: Cold temperatures can drain batteries quickly, so bring spares.

Important Note: Remember that the Northern Lights are a natural phenomenon, and sightings are not guaranteed. Patience and a bit of luck are key!

Outdoor Activities

Tromsø's stunning natural landscape provides the perfect setting for a wide range of outdoor adventures, whether you're visiting during the sun-drenched summer months or the snowy winter season.

Summer Activities

Hiking: Tromsø is a hiker's paradise, with trails ranging from easy strolls to challenging climbs.

Fløya Mountain:

- Sherpatrappa Stairs: Ascend (or descend) the Sherpatrappa, a staircase with approximately 1200 steps built by Nepalese Sherpas. It's a popular route with stunning views. Allow 1-2 hours for the descent.
- Fjellheisen Cable Car: Take the cable car to the top of Fløya for panoramic views and access to various trails. (Website: https://fjellheisen.no/en/](https://fjellheisen.no/en/))
- Other Trails: Explore trails like the "Varden" trail for a less crowded option.

Tromsdalstinden: (Experienced hikers only)

- The Challenge: Tromsø's highest peak (1238 meters) offers a demanding but rewarding hike. Allow 6-8 hours for the round trip.
- Route: The most common route starts from the Tromsdalen valley.
- Safety: Be prepared for steep sections, loose rocks, and changing weather.

Kvaløya Island:

- Coastal Trails: Hike along the coast for dramatic cliffs, sandy beaches, and views of the open sea.
- Ersfjordbotn: A popular starting point for hikes with options for all levels.
- Breivikeidet: Hike to the top of Store Blåmann (1044 meters) for spectacular fjord views.

Tips for Hiking:

- Essential Gear: Sturdy hiking boots, waterproof jacket, layers of clothing, map, compass or GPS, water, snacks.
- Safety First: Check the weather forecast, inform someone of your plans, and be aware of your limitations.
- Trail Etiquette: Stay on marked trails, pack out all trash, and respect wildlife.

Kayaking: Experience Tromsø from a different perspective by paddling through its picturesque fjords.

Guided Tours:

- Providers: Tromsø Activities ([https://tromsoactivities.com/] (https://www.google.com/url?sa=E&source=gmail&q=https://tromsoactivities.com/)), Arctic Guide Service ([https://www.arcticguideservice.no/)
- Options: Day trips, sunset tours, multi-day expeditions.
- Benefits: Learn about the area, improve kayaking skills, and enjoy a safe experience.

Rentals:

- Providers: Tromsø Outdoor (https://www.tromsooutdoor.no/), Kayak Tromsø
- Types: Single kayaks, double kayaks, sit-on-top kayaks.

Safety Tips:

- Wear a life jacket at all times.
- Dress for the water temperature, not the air temperature.
- Be aware of tides, currents, and weather conditions.
- Paddle with a buddy or inform someone of your kayaking plans.

Fishing: Tromsø's waters offer excellent fishing opportunities.

Fishing Trips:

- Providers: Arctic Fishing Adventures, Tromsø Havfiske
- Targets: Cod, haddock, coalfish, halibut, redfish.
- Experience: No experience necessary; all equipment is usually provided.

Shore Fishing:

- Popular Spots: Telegrafbukta beach, Grøtsund strait.
- Tips: Use local bait and tackle for the best results.

Licenses:

- Requirements: No license is required for saltwater fishing. Freshwater fishing may require a license.

Cycling: Explore Tromsø and its surroundings at your own pace on a bicycle.

Bike Rentals:

- Providers: Tromsø Outdoor, Arctic Rent a Bike
- Types: City bikes, mountain bikes, electric bikes, children's bikes.

Cycling Routes:

- Coastal Route: Cycle along the scenic coastal road towards Kvaløya Island.
- Island Exploration: Explore the quiet roads and trails of Kvaløya or Sommarøy Island.
- City Center: Cycle through the city center and along the harbor.

Tips:

- Wear a helmet and reflective clothing.
- Be aware of traffic and follow traffic rules.
- Plan your route and consider the terrain.

Winter Activities

Skiing and Snowboarding: Tromsø offers fantastic skiing and snowboarding opportunities with stunning Arctic scenery.

Tromsø Alpin Park:

- Location: On Fløya mountain, accessible by the Fjellheisen cable car.
- Slopes: Variety of slopes for all levels, from beginners to advanced skiers and snowboarders.
- Facilities: Ski lifts, ski school, equipment rental, café, restaurant.
- Night Skiing: Enjoy skiing under the floodlights with views of the city lights.

Lyngen Alps:

- Location: East of Tromsø, across the Ullsfjorden fjord.

- Terrain: More challenging slopes, off-piste skiing, and ski touring opportunities.
- Scenery: Known for its dramatic peaks, glaciers, and breathtaking fjord views.
- Getting There: Car, bus, or organized tours from Tromsø.
- Equipment Rental: Available at both ski resorts and various shops in Tromsø city center.

Snowshoeing: Explore the winter wonderland at your own pace with snowshoeing.

Trails:

- Marked Trails: Follow marked trails on Fløya mountain, Kvaløya Island, or in the Lyngen Alps.
- Off-the-Beaten-Path: Venture off the trails with a guide for a more adventurous experience.

Guided Tours:

- Providers: Tromsø Outdoor, Arctic Guide Service
- Benefits: Learn about the local flora and fauna, discover hidden gems, and enjoy a safe experience.

Rentals:

- Providers: Tromsø Outdoor, various sports shops in Tromsø.

Tips:

- Dress in warm layers, waterproof clothing, and sturdy winter boots.
- Use trekking poles for better balance and stability.
- Bring water and snacks.
- Be aware of avalanche risks in certain areas.

Dog Sledding: Experience the thrill of mushing your own team of huskies through the Arctic wilderness.

Tours:

- Duration: Range from short introductory rides to multi-day expeditions.

- Inclusions: Usually include transportation, warm clothing, instructions, and a meal.
- Providers: Tromsø Villmarkssenter Lyngen North ([https://lyngen.north/] (https://www.google.com/url?sa=E&source=gmail&q=https://lyngen.north/))

What to Expect:

- Learn how to handle a dog sled.
- Experience the power and enthusiasm of the huskies.
- Enjoy the peaceful scenery and the unique bond with the dogs.

Tips:

- Dress warmly in layers.
- Bring a camera to capture the unforgettable moments.
- Listen carefully to the instructions from the guides.

Reindeer Sledding: Enjoy a more relaxed pace and learn about Sami culture with a reindeer sledding experience.

Tours:

- Duration: Typically, 1-2 hours.
- Inclusions: Reindeer sledding, a visit to a Sami camp, storytelling, and traditional Sami food (like reindeer stew).
- Providers: Tromsø Arctic Reindeer ([https://www.tromsoarcticreindeer.com/] (https://www.tromsoarcticreindeer.com/))

What to Expect:

- Learn about reindeer herding and Sami traditions.
- Enjoy a peaceful ride through the snowy landscape.
- Interact with the reindeer and learn about their importance to the Sami people.

Tips:

- Dress warmly.
- Bring a camera to capture the experience.
- Ask questions and engage with the Sami guides.

Important Notes:

- Safety First: Always prioritize safety when participating in outdoor activities. Follow instructions from guides, wear appropriate clothing and equipment, and be aware of weather conditions.
- Guided Tours: Consider joining guided tours, especially if you're new to an activity or unfamiliar with the area. Guides can provide valuable insights, ensure your safety, and enhance your experience.
- Equipment Rental: Book equipment rentals in advance, especially during peak season.
- Respect the Environment: Follow Leave No Trace principles and respect the natural environment. Pack out any trash, stay on marked trails, and be mindful of wildlife.

Cultural Experiences

Tromsø offers a rich blend of history, art, and indigenous Sami culture, providing fascinating insights into life in the Arctic.

Museums:

Polar Museum:

- Focus: Explores the history of polar exploration, with exhibits on famous expeditions, Arctic hunting, and the lives of explorers like Roald Amundsen and Fridtjof Nansen.
- Highlights: Historic artifacts, photographs, and documents, a replica of Amundsen's polar cabin.
- Address: Søndre Tollbodgate 11, 9008 Tromsø

Tromsø University Museum:

- Focus: Covers a wide range of topics, including Sami culture, archaeology, natural history, and the Northern Lights.
- Highlights: Sami exhibits with traditional clothing and artifacts, a planetarium, and geological displays.
- Address: Lars Thørings veg 10, 9037 Tromsø

- Website: [https://uit.no/tmu] (https://www.google.com/url?sa=E&source=gmail&q=https://uit.no/tmu)

Art Museum of Northern Norway:

- Focus: Showcases Norwegian and international art, with a focus on artists from Northern Norway.
- Highlights: Paintings, sculptures, and installations by artists like Edvard Munch and Harriet Backer.
- Address: Sjøgata 1, 9008 Tromsø
- Website: [https://nnkm.no/en] (https://www.google.com/url?sa=E&source=gmail&q=https://nnkm.no/en)

Landmarks:

Arctic Cathedral:

- Architecture: Modern landmark with a distinctive A-frame design and beautiful stained-glass windows.
- Concerts: Often hosts concerts and events, especially during the Midnight Sun period.
- Address: Hans Nilsens veg 41, 9020 Tromsdalen
- Website: [https://www.ishavskatedralen.no/en/] (https://www.google.com/url?sa=E&source=gmail&q=https://www.ishavskatedralen.no/en/)

Tromsø Bridge:

- Iconic Structure: Cantilever bridge connecting Tromsdalen to the mainland, offering panoramic views of the city and surrounding mountains.
- Walking/Cycling: Pedestrian and cycle paths provide excellent vantage points.

Fjellheisen Cable Car:

- Panoramic Views: Ascend to the top of Fløya mountain for breathtaking views of Tromsø, the fjords, and the surrounding islands.
- Hiking: Access to hiking trails from the upper station.
- Restaurant: Enjoy a meal with a view at the Fjellstua restaurant.

- Address: Sollivegen 12, 9020 Tromsdalen
- Website: [https://fjellheisen.no/en/] (https://fjellheisen.no/en/)

Polaria (Arctic Aquarium):

- Arctic Wildlife: See bearded seals, harbor seals, and other Arctic marine life.

77

- Exhibits: Learn about the Arctic ecosystem, climate change, and polar research.
- Arctic Walkway: Experience a simulated Arctic environment with ice and snow.
- Address: Hjalmar Johansens gate 12, 9296 Tromsø
- Website: [https://polaria.no/en/] (https://www.google.com/url?sa=E&source=gmail&q=https://polaria.no/en/)

Sami Culture:

- Indigenous People: Learn about the Sami, the indigenous people of northern Scandinavia, their history, traditions, and connection to reindeer herding.
- Sami Experiences: Visit a Sami camp, try reindeer sledding, and learn about Sami handicrafts and storytelling.
- Tromsø Arctic Reindeer: Offers reindeer sledding, lavvu stays, and cultural experiences. ([https://www.tromsoarcticreindeer.com/] (https://www.tromsoarcticreindeer.com/))

Festivals and Events:

- Tromsø International Film Festival (TIFF): January - ([https://tiff.no/en/] (https://www.google.com/url?sa=E&source=gmail&q=https://tiff.no/en/))
- Northern Lights Festival: January/February
- Midnight Sun Marathon: June – ([https://msm.no/] (https://www.google.com/url?sa=E&source=gmail&q=https://msm.no/))
- Bukta Open Air Rock Festival: July
- Tromsø Arctic Pride: October

Day Trips and Excursions

Explore the breathtaking landscapes beyond Tromsø with these day trips and excursions:

Nearby Islands:

- Sommarøy: Known for its white-sand beaches, crystal-clear waters, and dramatic mountain scenery. Activities: kayaking, hiking, fishing, and enjoying the Midnight Sun in summer. (Accessible by car or bus.)
- Senja: Norway's second-largest island, offering stunning fjords, jagged peaks, fishing villages, and hiking trails. (Accessible by car, bus, or ferry.)

- Kvaløya: Explore the diverse landscapes of Kvaløya, with its mountains, fjords, beaches, and charming villages. (Accessible by car or bus.)

Fjords:

- Cruises: Take a fjord cruise to experience the majestic beauty of the surrounding fjords, with towering cliffs, waterfalls, and wildlife sightings.
- Providers: Tromsø Fjord Tours, Arctic Explorer

National Parks:

- Lyngen Alps National Park: Explore the dramatic landscapes of the Lyngen Alps, with glaciers, peaks, and valleys. Activities: hiking, skiing, and enjoying the Northern Lights in winter. (Accessible by car or organized tours.)

Important Notes:

- Transportation: Plan your transportation for day trips and excursions in advance. Consider renting a car for more flexibility, or book organized tours for convenience.
- Weather: Be prepared for changing weather conditions, especially on boat trips and in the mountains.
- Booking: Book tours and activities in advance, especially during peak season.

CHAPTER 6: LOCAL DINING

Top Restaurants

Tromsø's culinary scene is a delightful mix of traditional Norwegian fare, fresh seafood, and international flavors.

Fine Dining

Fiskekompaniet:

- Specialty: Seafood. Renowned for its exquisite seafood dishes featuring the freshest catches of the day, including king crab, scallops, and Arctic char.
- Atmosphere: Elegant and sophisticated with harbor views, perfect for a special occasion.
- Booking: Highly recommended, especially for dinner.
- Address: Killen greens gate 4, 9008 Tromsø
- Website: [https://www.fiskekompani.no/] (https://www.fiskekompani.no/)

Mathallen:

- Specialty: Modern Norwegian cuisine with Arctic ingredients. Tasting menus showcase seasonal flavors and innovative techniques.
- Atmosphere: Stylish and contemporary with an open kitchen, allowing diners to see the chefs at work.
- Booking: Recommended for dinner.
- Address: Grønnegata 58, 9008 Tromsø
- Website: [https://mathallentromso.no/] (https://mathallentromso.no/)

Emmas Drømmekjøkken:

- Specialty: Innovative Nordic cuisine with a focus on local and seasonal ingredients. Expect creative dishes and surprising flavor combinations.
- Atmosphere: Intimate and charming with a focus on culinary artistry.
- Booking: Essential, especially for weekend evenings.
- Address: Kirkegata 8, 9008 Tromsø

Mid-Range

Bardus Bistro:

- Specialty: Norwegian and European dishes with a modern twist. Known for its reindeer dishes, local seafood, and creative presentations.

- Atmosphere: Cozy and relaxed with a bistro-style setting, perfect for a casual yet refined dining experience.
- Booking: Recommended for dinner.
- Address: Cora Sandels gate 4, 9008 Tromsø
- Website: [https://bardus.no/] (https://bardus.no/)

Full Steam:

- Specialty: Seafood and local specialties served in a historic setting (a former fish factory). Offers a unique atmosphere and a taste of Tromsø's history.
- Atmosphere: Rustic and charming with a maritime theme.
- Booking: Recommended for dinner.
- Address: Strandtorget 1, 9008 Tromsø
- Website: [https://fullsteam.no/] (https://fullsteam.no/)

Restaurant Smak:

- Specialty: Seasonal Norwegian tasting menus with a focus on local produce. Offers a refined culinary journey through the region's flavors.
- Atmosphere: Small and intimate with a focus on the culinary experience.
- Booking: Essential.
- Address: Skippergata 17, 9008 Tromsø

Casual

Raketten:

- Specialty: Traditional Norwegian "pølse" (sausages) with various toppings. A local favorite for a quick and tasty meal.
- Atmosphere: Casual and lively, perfect for a quick bite or late-night snack.
- Address: Storgata 94, 9008 Tromsø

Casa Inferno:

- Specialty: Authentic Italian pizzas cooked in a wood-fired oven. Offers a wide variety of pizzas with fresh and flavorful toppings.
- Atmosphere: Relaxed and family-friendly.
- Booking: Recommended for larger groups.
- Address: Grønnegata 77, 9008 Tromsø
- Website: [https://casainferno.no/] (https://casainferno.no/)

Pastafabrikken:

- Specialty: Homemade pasta dishes with various sauces and toppings. Offers a comforting and satisfying meal with fresh, handmade pasta.
- Atmosphere: Casual and cozy with a focus on fresh ingredients.
- Address: Storgata 51, 9008 Tromsø

- Website: [https://pastafabrikken.no/] (https://pastafabrikken.no/)

Cafés and Bakeries

- Kaffebønna: Popular café with a wide selection of coffee, tea, and pastries. (Address: Storgata 103, 9008 Tromsø)
- Risø Mat & Kaffebar: Cozy café with delicious sandwiches, soups, and cakes. (Address: Storgata 52, 9008 Tromsø)
- Svermeri Kafe og Redesign: Charming café with homemade cakes, light lunches, and a focus on local ingredients. (Address: Grønnegata 81, 9008 Tromsø)

Tips for Dining in Tromsø:

- Reservations: Make reservations in advance, especially for popular restaurants and during peak season.
- Seafood: Don't miss the opportunity to try fresh, local seafood.
- Local Specialties: Sample traditional Norwegian dishes like reindeer stew (finnbiff), fish soup, and whale meat (if you're adventurous).
- Budget: Tromsø can be expensive, but there are options for all budgets. Look for lunch specials or try casual eateries.
- Tipping: Tipping is not expected but appreciated for good service.

Local Cuisine

Tromsø's location in the Arctic Circle heavily influences its cuisine. Expect fresh seafood, game meats, and hearty dishes designed to warm you up in the cold climate.

Reindeer Stew (Finnbiff): This traditional Sami dish is a flavorful stew made with tender reindeer meat, often simmered with bacon, onions, mushrooms, and a rich brown sauce. It's usually served with lingonberry jam and mashed potatoes.

- Where to Try: Bardus Bistro, Fiskekompaniet, Raketten (for a casual version)

Stockfish (Tørrfisk): Dried cod that has been preserved through a natural drying process. It has a unique, chewy texture and a concentrated flavor. Stockfish is often prepared with boiled potatoes, bacon, and butter.

- Where to Try: Fiskekompaniet, Full Steam

Fresh Seafood: Tromsø is a seafood lover's paradise! Enjoy fresh catches like cod, salmon, halibut, king crab, and prawns. Try them grilled, pan-fried, baked, or in a creamy fish soup.

- Where to Try: Fiskekompaniet (renowned for its seafood), Full Steam, Mathallen

Whale Meat: Whale meat is a traditional food in Norway, though it can be controversial. If you're curious, you can find it on some menus in Tromsø.

- Where to Try: Fiskekompaniet (occasionally), some traditional restaurants

Cloudberries (Multer): These golden-yellow berries grow in the Arctic and have a unique, tart flavor. They are often used in jams, desserts, and sauces.

- Where to Try: Look for cloudberry desserts at local cafés and bakeries.

Brunost (Brown Cheese): A caramelized whey cheese with a sweet and salty flavor. It's often served on bread or waffles for breakfast or as a snack.

- Where to Try: Most cafés and grocery stores.

Tips for Experiencing Local Cuisine:

- Don't be afraid to try new things! Tromsø offers a unique opportunity to sample flavors you won't find anywhere else.
- Ask for recommendations. Locals can point you to their favorite hidden gems.

- Visit the local markets. Tromsø has markets where you can find fresh produce, seafood, and local specialties.
- Consider a food tour. A guided food tour can be a great way to learn about the local cuisine and sample a variety of dishes.
- Enjoy the experience! Tromsø's culinary scene is a delicious adventure waiting to be explored.

CHAPTER 7: PRACTICAL TIPS

What to Pack

Tromsø's Arctic location and unique climate require some preparation to ensure a comfortable and enjoyable trip.

Year-Round

- Base Layers: Thermal underwear (tops and bottoms) made of merino wool or synthetic materials.
- Mid-Layers: Fleece jackets, wool sweaters, or down vests for added warmth.
- Outerwear: Waterproof and windproof jacket, preferably with a hood.
- Comfortable Pants: Jeans, hiking pants, or waterproof trousers.
- Warm Socks: Wool or synthetic socks for insulation.
- Sturdy Footwear: Waterproof hiking boots or winter boots with good grip.
- Accessories: Warm hat, gloves, scarf, sunglasses (even in winter, the sun can be strong when reflecting off snow).
- Essentials: Adapter (European plug), any necessary medications, toiletries.

Summer (June-August)

- Lighter Clothing: T-shirts, shorts, and a light jacket for cooler evenings.
- Rain Gear: A lightweight raincoat or umbrella.

- Swimsuit: If you plan on taking a dip in the fjords (brave!).
- Insect Repellent: Mosquitoes can be present in some areas.

Winter (November-March)

- Extra Layers: Pack more thermal layers and heavier sweaters.
- Warm Hat and Gloves: Consider a hat that covers your ears and waterproof gloves.
- Thermal Socks: Bring several pairs of thick, warm socks.
- Ice Grips: These can be helpful for walking on icy sidewalks.
- Headlamp: Useful for navigating in the dark during the Polar Night.

Weather and Safety

Tromsø experiences dramatic seasonal changes in weather and daylight hours.

Winter (November-March):

- Temperature: Averages between -4°C (25°F) and -7°C (19°F). Can drop to -20°C (-4°F) or lower.
- Conditions: Snow, ice, strong winds, and limited daylight hours (Polar Night).
- Northern Lights: Peak viewing season.

Spring (April-May):

- Temperature: Gradually warming up with increasing daylight hours.
- Conditions: Snow melt, some rain, and unpredictable weather.

Summer (June-August):

- Temperature: Averages around 12°C (54°F) but can reach 25°C (77°F) on sunny days.
- Conditions: Mild temperatures, long daylight hours (Midnight Sun), and occasional rain.

Autumn (September-October):

- Temperature: Cooling down with decreasing daylight hours.
- Conditions: Rain, wind, and the first snowfall.

Winter Hazards:

- Ice and Snow: Be cautious when walking on icy sidewalks and roads. Use ice grips for better traction.
- Strong Winds: Be prepared for strong winds, especially in coastal areas.
- Limited Visibility: During the Polar Night, visibility can be very low. Use caution when walking or driving.

General Safety:

- Emergency Contacts: 112 (general emergencies), 113 (police), 110 (fire).
- Wildlife: Be aware of wildlife such as reindeer, moose, and polar bears (rarely seen near Tromsø).
- Outdoor Activities: Follow safety guidelines and instructions from guides, especially during winter activities.
- Valuables: Keep your valuables secure and be aware of pickpockets in crowded areas.

By being prepared for Tromsø's weather and following these safety tips, you can ensure a safe and enjoyable trip to this Arctic wonderland.

Local Transportation

Buses:

- Operator: Troms fylkestrafikk (Troms County Transport)

Routes: An extensive network of bus routes covers the city center, residential areas, and surrounding villages. Key routes include:

- Route 20: Connects the airport to the city center and continues to the university.

- Route 24: Travels along the eastern side of the island, passing through Tromsdalen and connecting to the cable car.
- Route 34: Circular route that connects the city center with major residential areas.
- Route 40 and 42: Serve the western side of the island, including popular destinations like Telegrafbukta beach.

Frequency: Buses generally run every 15-30 minutes on main routes, with more frequent service during peak hours (7:00 AM – 9:00 AM and 3:00 PM – 5:00 PM). Less frequent service on evenings and weekends.

Schedules:

- Website: [https://www.tromskortet.no/] (https://www.google.com/url?sa=E&source=gmail&q=https://www.tromskortet.no/)
- Troms Mobillett App: Download the app for journey planning, ticket purchases, and real-time bus tracking.
- Bus Stops: Most bus stops have posted timetables.

Tickets:

- Troms Mobillett App: The most convenient option. Purchase single tickets, day passes, period passes, and more.

- On Board: You can purchase single tickets from the bus driver (cash only, Norwegian Krone). Be prepared with the exact fare as drivers may not provide change.
- Ticket Machines: Ticket machines are available at some major bus stops and the main bus terminal (Tromsø Rutebilstasjon).

Travel Cards:

- Troms Travelcard: Offers unlimited travel on buses and ferries within a specified zone and time period (24 hours, 72 hours, 7 days).
- Value Card: Load a value card with credit and use it to pay for individual journeys at a discounted rate.

Ferries:

Routes: Ferries connect Tromsø to nearby islands and communities. Some key routes:

- Tromsø – Kvaløya: Frequent ferries connect the city center to various points on Kvaløya Island.
- Tromsø – Sommarøy: Ferries operate to Sommarøy Island, known for its beautiful beaches.
- Tromsø – Lyngen: Ferries cross the Ullsfjorden fjord to the Lyngen Alps.

Operators:

- Torghatten Nord: Operates most of the ferries in the region. (Website: https://www.torghatten-nord.no/
- Bjørklids Ferjer: Operates some smaller ferry routes.

Tickets:

- Online: Purchase tickets online in advance on the ferry operator's website.
- Ferry Terminals: Ticket offices are located at the ferry terminals.
- On Board: On some routes, you can purchase tickets directly from the ferry staff.

Other Transportation Options

Taxis:

- Availability: Taxis are readily available in the city center, especially near hotels, restaurants, and popular attractions.
- Hailing: You can hail taxis on the street, but it's more common to book them in advance.
- Taxi Ranks: Taxi ranks are located at Tromsø Airport (TOS), the main bus terminal (Tromsø Rutebilstasjon), and near major hotels.

Booking:

- Taxi Apps: Use taxi apps like Tromsø Taxi or Mivai.
- Phone: Call Tromsø Taxi (+47 07777) or Din Taxi (+47 03011).
- Fares: Taxis are metered, and fares are regulated. Expect higher fares during evenings (after 6:00 PM), weekends, and public holidays.
- Payment: Most taxis accept credit cards, but it's always good to have some Norwegian Krone on hand.

Bicycles:

Rentals: Rent bicycles from various providers:

- Tromsø Outdoor: Offers a wide range of bikes, including city bikes, mountain bikes, and electric bikes. (Website:

[https://www.tromsooutdoor.no/]
(https://www.tromsooutdoor.no/))
- Arctic Rent a Bike: Located near the harbor, offering city bike rentals.
- Cycling Paths: Tromsø has a network of dedicated cycling paths, particularly along the waterfront and in residential areas.

Safety:

- Helmet: Wearing a helmet is recommended.
- Lights: Use bike lights, especially during the darker months.
- Traffic Rules: Follow traffic rules and be aware of pedestrians and other cyclists.

Tips for Getting Around:

- Plan Your Routes: Use the Troms Mobillett app or the Troms fylkestrafikk website to plan your bus journeys and check schedules.
- Validate Your Ticket: Remember to validate your ticket when boarding the bus by scanning it on the validation machine.
- Consider a Travel Card: If you plan to use public transportation frequently, a Troms Travelcard can offer cost savings and convenience.
- Walking: Tromsø city center is compact and walkable. Enjoy exploring the city on foot.

- Airport Transfers: The Flybussen airport express bus provides frequent service between Tromsø Airport (TOS) and the city center.
- Ferry Travel: Book ferry tickets in advance, especially during peak season or for popular routes, as ferries can fill up quickly.

Useful Phrases in Norwegian

Basics

- Hello: Hei (pronounced "hay")
- Goodbye: Ha det (pronounced "hah deh")
- Yes: Ja (pronounced "yah")
- No: Nei (pronounced "nay")
- Please: Vær så snill (pronounced "vehr soh snill")
- Thank you: Takk (pronounced "tahk")
- You're welcome: Vær så god (pronounced "vehr soh goh")
- Excuse me: Unnskyld (pronounced "oon-shil")

Greetings

- Good morning: God morgen (pronounced "goo morn")
- Good day: God dag (pronounced "goo dahg")
- Good evening: God kveld (pronounced "goo kvell")
- Good night: God natt (pronounced "goo natt")

Useful Phrases

- How are you? Hvordan har du det? (pronounced "voor-dan har doo deh?")
- I'm fine, thank you: Jeg har det bra, takk (pronounced "yay har deh brah, tahk")
- Do you speak English? Snakker du engelsk? (pronounced "snak-ker doo eng-elsk?")
- I don't understand: Jeg forstår ikke (pronounced "yay for-storr ik-keh")
- Please speak slowly: Vær så snill å snakke sakte (pronounced "vehr soh snill oh snak-keh sak-the")
- Where is the [toilet/bus stop/train station]? Hvor er [toalettet/bussholdeplassen/togstasjonen]? (pronounced "voor er [too-a-let-the/buss-hol-deh-plass-en/tog-stah-shoo-nen]?")
- How much does this cost? Hvor mye koster dette? (pronounced "voor mee-yeh kost-er det-the?")

Dining

- I would like to order: Jeg vil gjerne bestille (pronounced "yay vill gjer-neh be-still-eh")
- The bill, please: Regningen, vær så snill (pronounced "reg-ning-en, vehr soh snill")
- Delicious! Deilig! (pronounced "day-lig")

Numbers

- One: En (pronounced "en")
- Two: To (pronounced "too")
- Three: Tre (pronounced "treh")
- Four: Fire (pronounced "fee-reh")
- Five: Fem (pronounced "fem")

Tips for Using Norwegian Phrases:

- Pronunciation: Norwegian pronunciation can be tricky. Listen to audio recordings or ask a local to help you with pronunciation.
- Politeness: Norwegians appreciate politeness. Use "vær så snill" (please) and "takk" (thank you) frequently.
- Effort: Even if your Norwegian isn't perfect, locals will appreciate your effort to communicate in their language.
- Smile: A smile goes a long way in any language!

CHAPTER 9: BONUS

Map Guides

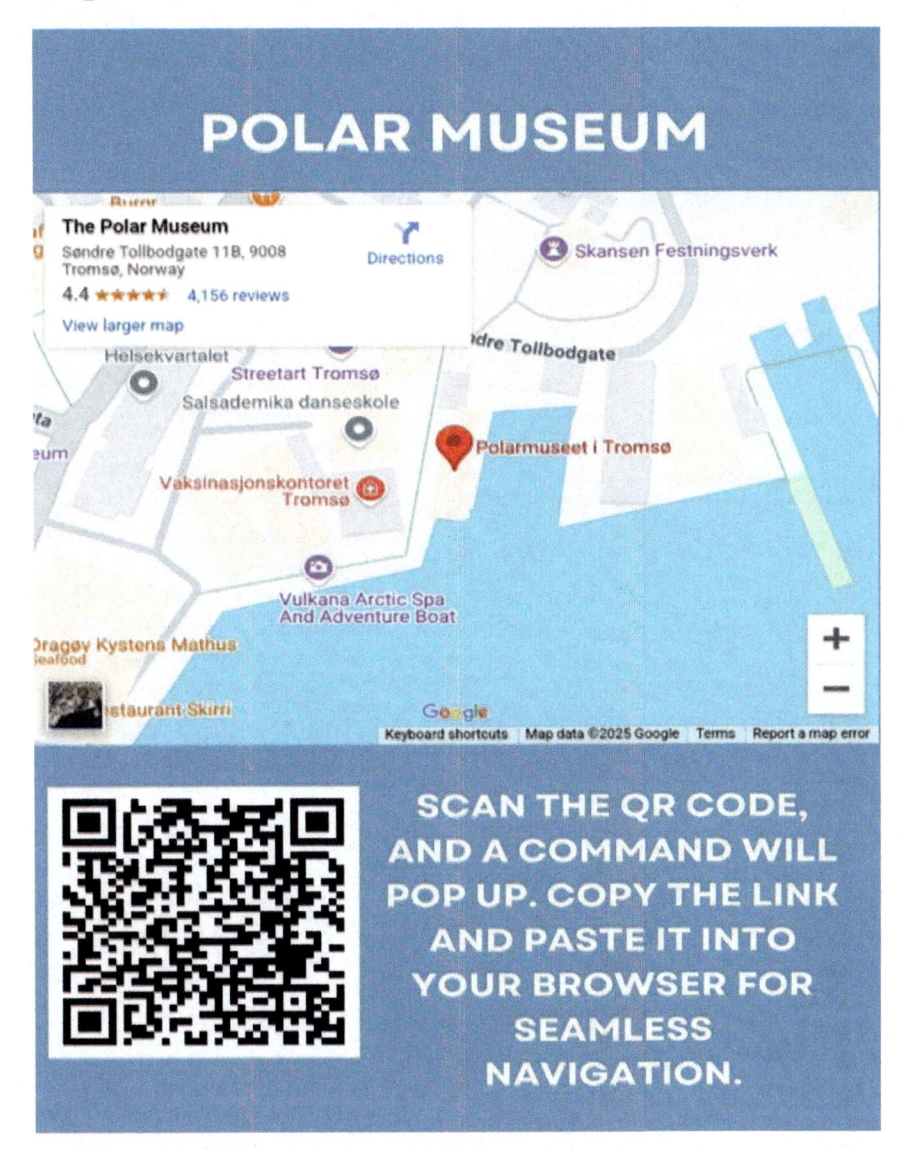

POLAR MUSEUM

The Polar Museum
Søndre Tollbodgate 11B, 9008 Tromsø, Norway
4.4 ★★★★★ 4,156 reviews
View larger map

SCAN THE QR CODE, AND A COMMAND WILL POP UP. COPY THE LINK AND PASTE IT INTO YOUR BROWSER FOR SEAMLESS NAVIGATION.

ARCTIC CATHEDRAL

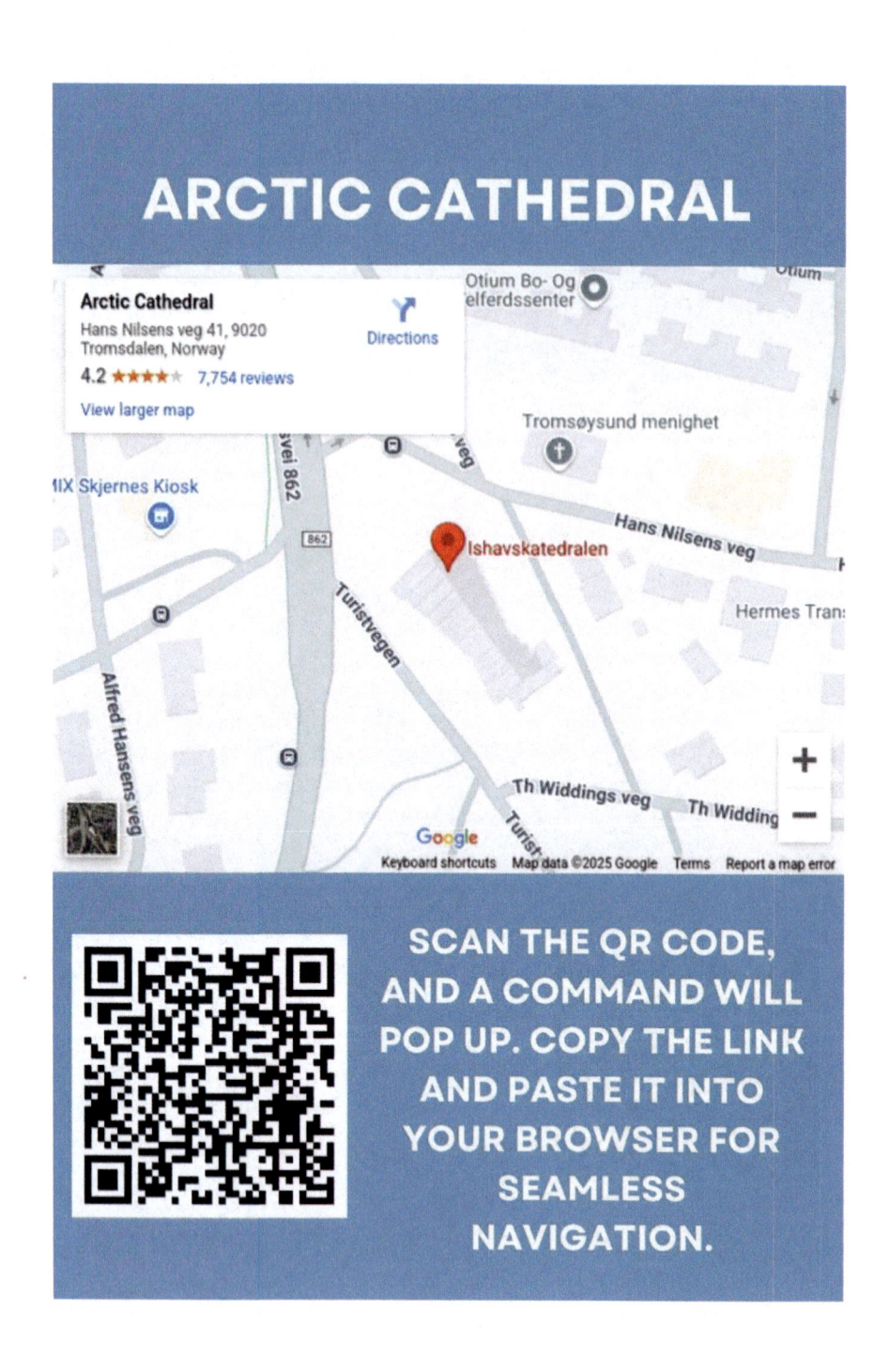

Arctic Cathedral
Hans Nilsens veg 41, 9020
Tromsdalen, Norway
4.2 ★★★★ 7,754 reviews
View larger map

SCAN THE QR CODE, AND A COMMAND WILL POP UP. COPY THE LINK AND PASTE IT INTO YOUR BROWSER FOR SEAMLESS NAVIGATION.

TROMSØ BRIDGE

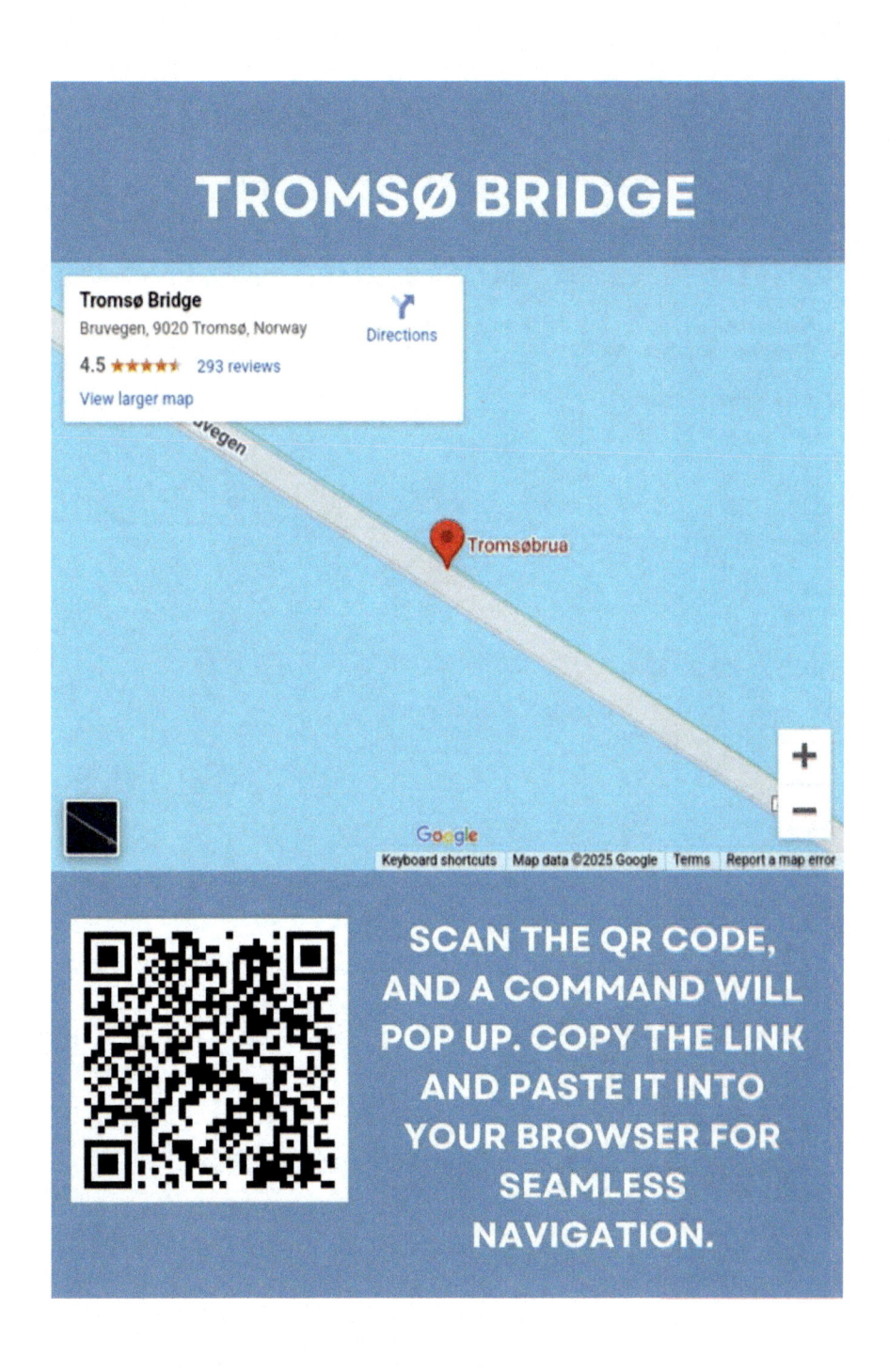

Tromsø Bridge
Bruvegen, 9020 Tromsø, Norway
4.5 ★★★★★ 293 reviews
View larger map

Directions

SCAN THE QR CODE, AND A COMMAND WILL POP UP. COPY THE LINK AND PASTE IT INTO YOUR BROWSER FOR SEAMLESS NAVIGATION.

FJELLHEISEN CABLE CAR

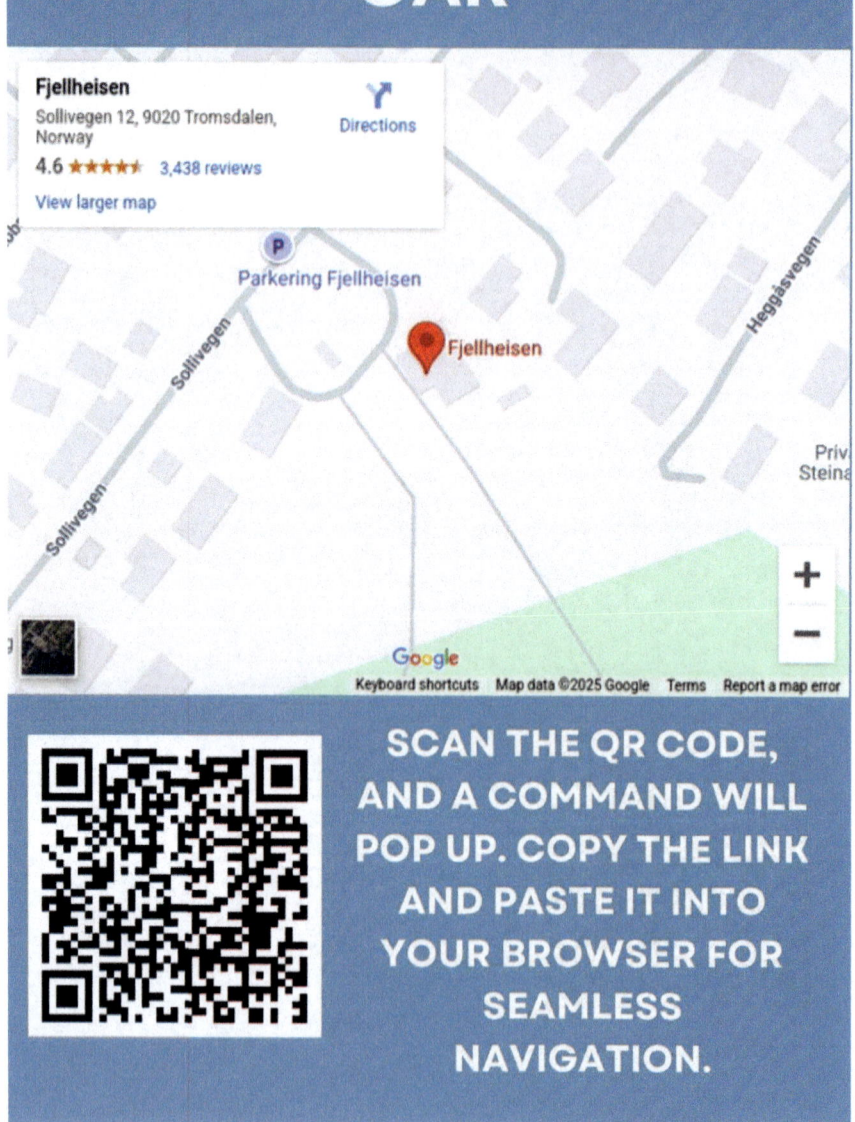

Fjellheisen
Sollivegen 12, 9020 Tromsdalen, Norway
4.6 ★★★★★ 3,438 reviews
View larger map

Directions

SCAN THE QR CODE, AND A COMMAND WILL POP UP. COPY THE LINK AND PASTE IT INTO YOUR BROWSER FOR SEAMLESS NAVIGATION.

POLARIA (ARCTIC AQUARIUM)

Polaria aquarium
Hjalmar Johansens gate 12, 9007 Tromsø, Norway
4.1 ★★★★★ 5,496 reviews
View larger map

SCAN THE QR CODE, AND A COMMAND WILL POP UP. COPY THE LINK AND PASTE IT INTO YOUR BROWSER FOR SEAMLESS NAVIGATION.

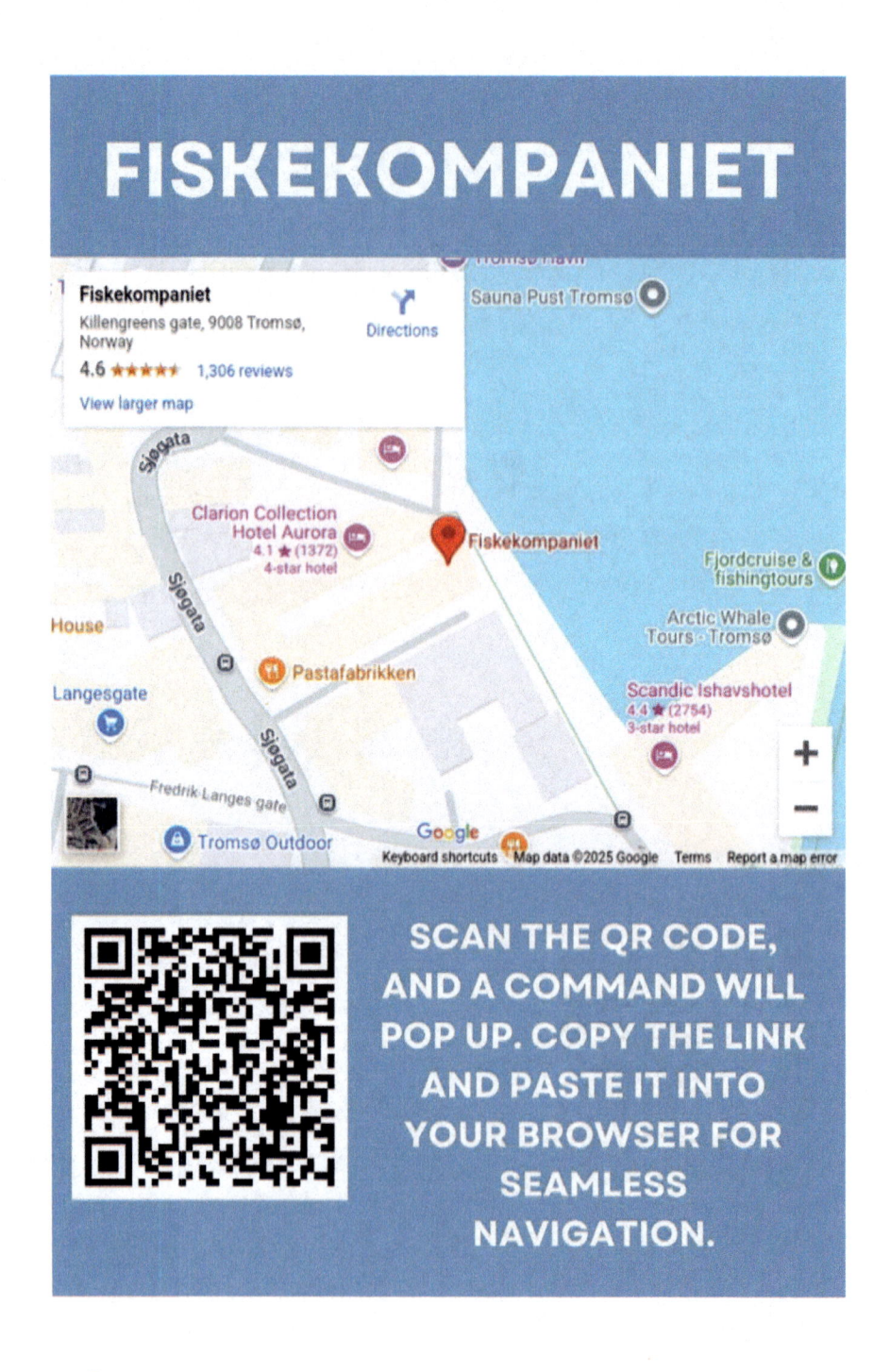

FISKEKOMPANIET

Fiskekompaniet
Killengreens gate, 9008 Tromsø, Norway
4.6 ★★★★★ 1,306 reviews
View larger map

SCAN THE QR CODE, AND A COMMAND WILL POP UP. COPY THE LINK AND PASTE IT INTO YOUR BROWSER FOR SEAMLESS NAVIGATION.

PRESTVANNET LAKE

Prestvannet
9011 Tromsø, Norway
4.5 ★★★★☆ 77 reviews
View larger map
Directions

SCAN THE QR CODE, AND A COMMAND WILL POP UP. COPY THE LINK AND PASTE IT INTO YOUR BROWSER FOR SEAMLESS NAVIGATION.

TROMSØ ICE DOMES

Tromsø Ice Domes
Tamokveien 1374, 9334 Øverbygd, Norway
4.6 ★★★★★ 557 reviews
View larger map

SCAN THE QR CODE, AND A COMMAND WILL POP UP. COPY THE LINK AND PASTE IT INTO YOUR BROWSER FOR SEAMLESS NAVIGATION.

KVALØYA ISLAND

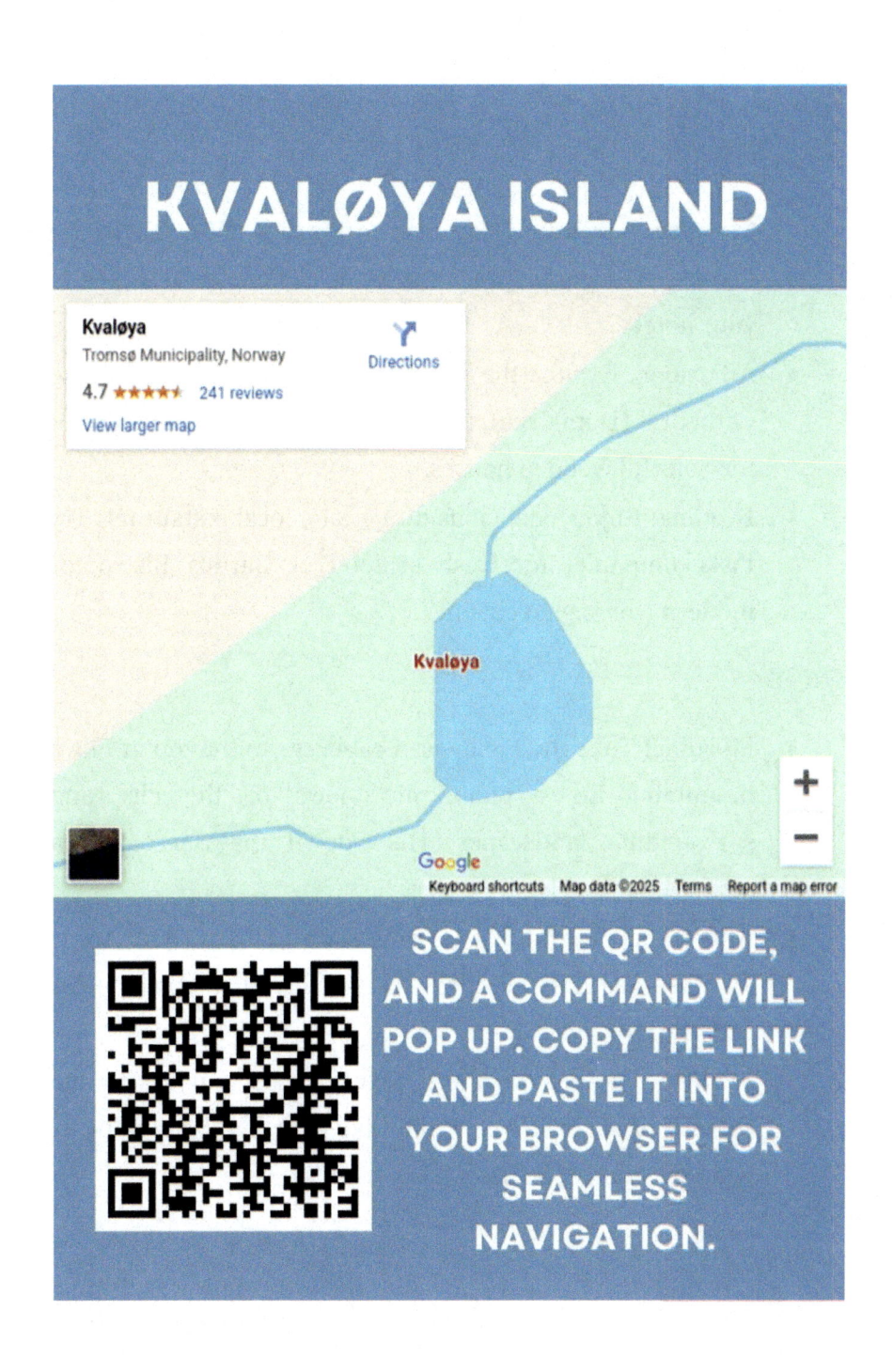

Kvaløya
Tromsø Municipality, Norway
4.7 ★★★★★ 241 reviews
View larger map

Directions

Kvaløya

Keyboard shortcuts | Map data ©2025 | Terms | Report a map error

SCAN THE QR CODE, AND A COMMAND WILL POP UP. COPY THE LINK AND PASTE IT INTO YOUR BROWSER FOR SEAMLESS NAVIGATION.

One week Itinerary

Day 1:

- Morning: Arrive at Tromsø Airport (TOS). Take the Flybussen airport express bus to the city center. Check in to your hotel.
- Afternoon: Explore the city center on foot. Visit the Tromsø Cathedral (Domkirke), stroll along the harbor, and admire the colorful wooden houses.
- Evening: Enjoy a delicious dinner at a local restaurant. Try Fiskekompaniet for fresh seafood or Bardus Bistro for modern Norwegian cuisine.

Day 2:

- Morning: Take the Fjellheisen cable car to the top of Fløya mountain. Enjoy panoramic views of the city and surrounding landscapes. Hike down the Sherpatrappa stairs.
- Afternoon: Visit the Polaria museum and learn about Arctic wildlife. See the bearded seals and learn about polar exploration.
- Evening: Join a Northern Lights chase tour (if it's the season) or relax at a cozy pub like Ølhallen, known for its wide selection of beers.

Day 3:

- Morning: Choose your adventure:
- Active: Go dog sledding or snowmobiling in the Arctic wilderness.
- Cultural: Visit the Tromsø University Museum and learn about Sami culture and Arctic history.
- Relaxing: Enjoy a leisurely breakfast and explore the shops and cafes in the city center.
- Afternoon: Visit the Arctic Cathedral (Ishavskatedralen), a stunning landmark with unique architecture. Attend a concert or service if available.
- Evening: Have dinner at a restaurant with local specialties. Try Full Steam for a historic setting or Mathallen for modern Norwegian cuisine.

Day 4:

- Day Trip: Take a day trip to one of the nearby islands:
- Kvaløya: Explore the island's diverse landscapes, hike to Ersfjordbotn, or visit the charming fishing villages.
- Sommarøy: Relax on the sandy beaches (in summer), go kayaking, or hike to the top of Hillesøy for stunning views.
- Evening: Enjoy a traditional Norwegian dinner at your chosen destination.

Day 5:

- Morning: Visit the Tromsø Ice Domes (seasonal) and experience the magic of a hotel made entirely of ice.
- Afternoon: Go shopping for souvenirs at the local shops. Look for Sami handicrafts, woolen sweaters, and local delicacies.
- Evening: Have a farewell dinner at a restaurant of your choice.

Day 6:

- Morning: Enjoy a relaxing breakfast and pack your bags.
- Afternoon: Visit any remaining attractions or museums you haven't had a chance to see.
- Evening: Depart from Tromsø Airport (TOS).

CONCLUSION

As your journey through the pages of this Tromsø Travel Guide comes to an end, we hope you feel inspired and well-equipped to embark on your own Arctic adventure.

Whether you're drawn to the mesmerizing dance of the Northern Lights, the thrill of outdoor activities, the charm of the city's culture, or the flavors of its cuisine, Tromsø has something to offer every traveler.

We've strived to provide you with accurate, up-to-date information and insightful tips to help you make the most of your time in this captivating city. From practical advice on transportation and accommodation to recommendations for unforgettable experiences and hidden gems, we've aimed to be your trusted companion on this journey of discovery.

As you prepare to explore the Arctic wonders of Tromsø, remember to embrace the spirit of adventure, respect the natural environment, and immerse yourself in the local culture. Allow yourself to be captivated by the magic of the Arctic, and create memories that will last a lifetime.

We hope this travel guide has been a valuable resource in planning your trip to Tromsø. We're always looking for ways to improve and provide the best possible information for our readers.

If you've used this guide during your travels, we would be grateful if you could share your honest feedback. Did you find the information helpful? Were there any aspects you particularly enjoyed? Your insights will help us make future editions even better.

Thank you for choosing Tromsø as your destination, and we wish you safe and unforgettable travels!

Happy Exploring!